Praise for *A Fork*

"I AM IN "PASSIONATE AGREEMENT" *with the authors! It is so important to start the critical career thinking process early. Not only do the skills the authors offer help with professional decision-making, they are basic ongoing life skills as well. Vital ingredients for healthy futures."* — **Dr. Beverly Kaye**, CEO, Beverly Kaye Associates, and author of *Up Is Not the Only Way* and *Love 'Em or Lose 'Em*

"IF ONLY I'D HAD SUCH A GREAT ROAD MAP *in the early days of my career."* — **Bob Rosner**, internationally syndicated career columnist and author of the bestselling *Boss's Survival Guide*

"ONE OF HIGH SCHOOL'S *greatest failings is its ignoring of anything related to careers. A Fork in the Road can really help."* — **Marty Nemko**, Ph.D., Career and Education Coach; Producer, host "Work With Marty Nemko" (NPR-San Francisco); Author, *Cool Careers for Dummies*; Columnist, Monster.com, *San Francisco Chronicle*

"AN ENGAGING WORKBOOK *that makes you ask the important questions to find your strengths and pick the right career. Filled with thought-provoking questions and examples from real-life, this is a must-have for all students who have questions about their future."* — **Kelly Tanabe**, author of *Get Into Any College* and *Get Free Cash for College*

"AN ENTERTAINING AND THOUGHT-PROVOKING BOOK *that involves the young adult reader on a ride toward their future. The skills gained almost effortlessly along the way are sure to become the foundation from which the reader can make compatible career decisions after college and beyond. The authors have front row seats in the subject area and communicate their knowledge with ease."* — **Shary Price**, PrepWorks Publishing, Publisher of *Tuning In To My Future: A Middle School Career Exploration Program*

"THE BOOK HELPED ME *organize my skills and interests, then unveiled many career opportunities that fit."* — **John Robert Frankfurt**, 18, Palo Alto High School Senior

"A WONDERFUL RESOURCE FOR YOUNG ADULTS. *The authors demonstrate their years of experience in the field."* — **Lance Choy**, Director, Career Development Center, Stanford University

"A GREAT RESOURCE FOR OUR STUDENTS. *Not only does it help them make important career decisions, but more importantly, it reinforces the need to start early in the career planning process."* — **Veda Swift Jeffries**, Assistant Director, Career Development Center, Stanford University

A Fork
in the Road

A CAREER PLANNING GUIDE FOR YOUNG ADULTS

Susan Maltz
Barbara Grahn

IMPACT PUBLICATIONS
Manassas Park, Virginia

Library of Congress Cataloguing-in-Publication Data

Maltz, Susan
    A Fork in the Road: A Career Planning Guide for Young Adults / Susan Maltz and Barbara Grahn
      p. cm.
      Includes index.
      ISBN 1-57023-197-4   2002114023

Publisher: For information on Impact Publications, including current and forthcoming publications, authors, press kits, online bookstore, and submission requirements, visit our website: www.impactpublications.com.

Publicity/Rights: For information on publicity, author interviews, and subsidiary rights, contact the Media Relations Department: Tel. 703-361-7300, Fax 703-335-9486, or email: info@impactpublications.com.

Sales/Distribution: All bookstore sales are handled through Impact's trade distributor: National Book Network, 15200 NBN Way, Blue Ridge Summit, PA 17214, Tel. 1-800-462-6420. All other sales and distribution inquiries should be directed to the publisher: Sales Department, IMPACT PUBLICATIONS, 9104 Manassas Drive, Suite N, Massassas Park, VA 20111-5211, Tel. 703-361-7300, Fax 703-335-9486, or email: info@impactpublications.com.

Illustrations by Barbara Grahn and Juan Vega.
Pencil graphic courtesy of www.mcmannis.com.
C1973.Illustration adapted from original by Dee Molenaar with permission of the publisher from "Cascade Alpine Guide" Volume 1 by Fred Beckey, The Mountaineers, Seattle, WA.

Contents

Acknowledgments

Many thanks to our student testers: Adrienne, Cori, John Robert, Katy, Matt, and Rick from Palo Alto High School, and Jim Burke's sophomore ACCESS class at Burlingame High School who gave us superb feedback. To our reviewers, Valerie Beeman, Sandra Clewans, Richard Michaels, and Lisa Rosenthal who edited and shaped our book—we could not have done it without you!

We would also like to thank our families for their support during this project, and Wally Amos for his advice and inspirational messages.

Last, but not least, appreciation and thanks to the many people who shared their knowledge and support of Susan's career-self management program at Stanford University.

Susan and Barbara

Introduction

After spending a combined 50+ years in the workplace and talking to thousands of young people it became clear to us that there is a lack of information on career self-management for young adults. So many young people are pressured to make career choices and set goals before they are ready, and without the tools they need to make an informed decision. When things don't work out, they often feel lost. When a young person has the tools and opportunity to make an informed career choice, the results in personal and professional growth can be phenomenal.

Many years ago, Susan counseled a young medical student who didn't want to be a doctor. He was terrified of calling his parents to let them know he wanted to drop out of medical school. Together, they talked a great deal about his life. His great passion was photography and he was pursuing this in his spare time. He never saw the connection between his love for photography and science. Once he realized that he could combine both in a career, he was ecstatic. He survived telling his parents that he didn't want to be a doctor and became a very successful medical photographer.

There are thousands of jobs available, yet most young adults are exposed to fewer than 100 of these. It's important to explore all career options, to keep an open mind, to know what you want, and learn how to get there.

The career self-management skills taught in this book can be used throughout your life. Reading and using this book is just the first step to finding a fulfilling career that you love.

Foreword

Sometimes all the planning in the world takes you down a road you least expect. A combination of motivation, circumstance, and serendipity can propel you to a career that exceeds your expectations. Here's what Wally Amos has to say about his unexpected career path:

Wally Amos: On the Road to Success

Why is it that we have such a fascination with being in control and having every aspect of life be perfect - creating great strategies on how we think our life should be?

I give many lectures, so I often get the opportunity to review my life. The major life-changing decisions in my life have not been planned. Instead they were wonderful, serendipitous experiences that always led to something better than what I had in mind.

Who would have thought that, 27 years after my parents divorced, I would make my mark selling chocolate chip cookies? But that's exactly what happened after I moved to New York to live with my Aunt Della at the tender age of 12.

Recently, I had a conversation with a friend who is one of the world's most respected heart surgeons. I asked him why he became a doctor. He said the only way he could get out of going to the college his family wanted him to attend, which specialized in engineers, was to become a doctor and attend a different school. That single unplanned decision altered the entire course of his life, and the lives of many others.

The following poem, "The Road to Success," which I received via e-mail, does a good job of describing how life works:

> The road to success is not straight. There is a curve called failure, a loop called confusion, speed bumps called friends, caution lights called family, and you will have flats called jobs. But if you have a spare called determination, an engine called perseverance and insurance called faith, you will make it to a place called success.

Add to that preparation, discipline, focus and enthusiasm, and you are on the road to success!

Wally Amos is founder of Uncle Wally's Muffin Company and author of *The Cookie Never Crumbles: Inspirational Recipes for Everyday Living*, St. Martin's Press, 2001. Printed with permission by the author.

Son, we're sending you on a road trip!

1

You're in the Driver's Seat

Are there so many career choices out there
you don't know which to choose?

Do you know what skills you will need
to launch your desired career?

Do you know what career is ideal for you?

Do you know what careers suit your style
and how to pursue them?

Not yet? Then this book is for you! Waking up each morning excited about your career is everyone's dream. Jump in and explore the world of career planning!

Have a pencil ready—it will be a key tool on your journey to success

The World of Work in the New Millennium

The world of work has changed dramatically in the last 20 years. There are many jobs that no longer exist and an abundance of newly created jobs for our high-tech world. Jobs are ever-changing and the job market has shifted dramatically.

What jobs or volunteer positions do your parents have?

_____

_____

_____

_____

What types of jobs do your parents' friends have?

_____

_____

_____

_____

Here are some interesting new jobs today:

Plant Geneticist – using biotech tools, introduces proteins into plants that can be used to fight human viruses.

Virtual Reality Architect – explores unbuilt designs using computers.

Nanotechnologist – makes machines at a molecular scale; creates virus-size robots using carbon fibers stronger than steel.

Business Process Analyst – determines and implements the best process to enhance the function of databases, computer systems, or other business applications.

Organizational Development Specialist – helps companies or departments perform at their best by enhancing or changing employee practices, work processes, the environment, culture, or structure.

Bioinformatics Analyst – a profession pairing biology and computer science; data produced by the Human Genome Project (gene sorting) is analyzed and studied for possible clues and eventual cures for diseases.

These are just a few of the hot new jobs in this millennium. The number of new job titles increases daily! Keep an open mind as you explore your options because the jobs of yesterday may not exist tomorrow.

It Takes Planning!

Key Point ⚷

Developing a plan or road map of what you want to do with your life is a crucial first step in finding work that you will enjoy for many years to come.

Students who graduate in the year 2003 will have approximately three to eight *career* changes in their life, and may have even more jobs. To top that off, 70 percent of today's jobs will disappear by the year 2050. So the job you may be thinking of today may not exist years from now.

What can you do about this? It is crucial that you become flexible and gain skills that will benefit you for the jobs of tomorrow. If you can think and plan globally early on in the career-planning process, the choice jobs can be yours. So don't just choose a job title and leave it at that. Mapping out your direction is important to starting down the right road. With the right map, you can end up with the needed skills to continue job exploration throughout your entire life.

Here are some of the new skills needed for the 21st century:

- ❖ Communication (good verbal and writing skills; computer literate; and fluency in a second language)

- ❖ Problem-solving (take initiative and seek solutions)

- ❖ Participating in work teams (work well and cooperatively with others)

❖ Continuous learning (keeping skills current and learning additional skills, leading to increased flexibility)

Typically, with each new job, you will build or enhance your skills. Self-assessment (knowing yourself) and continuous skill building are key steps in choosing a career that's right for you.

What skills do you already have? Do you think that you have no skills at all? Starting out with no core skills to perform a job is rare. Everyone has skills, although some may have more developed skills than others. Skills are acquired abilities to do something through practice or training. Think about what you are good at today and write those things on the lines below. Here are some examples:

Writing	Fixing things	Explaining
Designing things	Solving problems	Leading a group
Speaking in public	Organizing events	Organizing people

My Skills:

_____

_____

_____

_____

Many of these skills are needed for the jobs of today and most likely will be needed for the jobs of tomorrow. Keep your skills in mind when you start Chapter 4 on skill identification.

Beginning to Plan

This book, designed as an interactive guide, helps you map your direction. Each section contains activities to help you find out more about your interests, skills, motivation, values, and working style, and help you explore the options available to you when choosing a career.

When you are exploring your career choices, it's important to begin your planning by thinking big and then narrowing down your options. The Career Self-Management World Map on the next page will help you identify the areas you need to explore. As you embark on your career journey, choose a place to start, but know that at any time in your life you can re-enter the career planning process and continue your journey around the World Map. The section called "Know Who You Are" is a good place to begin. It is important to learn about yourself and what you have to offer the world.

The first six chapters of this book focus on knowing who you are:

- ❖ Your values
- ❖ Your interests
- ❖ Your skills
- ❖ Your accomplishments
- ❖ Your working style
- ❖ Your passions and motivation

Chapters 6 and 8 focus on exploring the world of work:

- ❖ How to research careers
- ❖ Explore work environments
- ❖ Explore lifestyles
- ❖ Conduct informational interviews

Chapters 7 and 8 help you evaluate your choices:

- ❖ Make decisions
- ❖ Set goals
- ❖ Get the necessary education and training
- ❖ Do reality testing
- ❖ Listen to yourself and others

Chapter 9 provides you with tools to reach your career destination:

- ❖ Write an action plan
- ❖ Make contacts
- ❖ Create resumes
- ❖ Write cover letters
- ❖ Prepare for interviews

Career Self-Management World Map

Know Who You Are
- Values
- Interests
- Skills
- Accomplishments
- Working Style
- Passion(s)
- Motivation

Explore Careers
- Research Careers
- Work Environments
- Lifestyles
- Conduct Informational Interviews

Reach Your Career Destination
- Action Plan
- Make Contacts
- Resumes
- Letters
- Interviews

Evaluate Your Choices
- Make Decisions
- Set Goals
- Get Necessary Education & Training
- Do Reality Testing
- Listen to Yourself and Others

The world is round and the place which may seem like the end may also be only the beginning.

– Ivy Baker Priest

Know Yourself

Key Point 🔑

Getting to know yourself is the only way to choose the right career for YOU.

Be ready with a pencil to complete the activities in each chapter. This book will help you identify the interests, skills, values, and preferences that will enable you to know yourself better. Once you know who you are, it will be easier to choose a career direction that fits.

Knowing yourself includes identifying your values or personal standards. For example:

❖ Do you want a job where you make lots of money?
❖ Do you prefer to work outdoors or inside?
❖ Do you prefer to work regular or flexible hours?
❖ Do you want a job helping others?

It's important to prioritize your values to help you choose a career that best fits you.

Knowing yourself also includes identifying your interests and preferences:

❖ Do you like working with people, or would you rather work with machines?
❖ Do you like working with data or files, or would you prefer to work with ideas?

It's important to know what you prefer, so that the job you choose reflects your interests.

After you've identified your values and interests, be sure to identify your skills. For example:

❖ Are you good at talking to people?
❖ Are you good at fixing machines?
❖ Can you organize an event flawlessly?

Knowing your skills will help you decide on a job and improve your chances for success. Your working style, motivation, and passion will also play a part in your career choice.

The next few chapters will help you get to know yourself better. After you have identified who you are, it will be time to explore job options that fit with your skills, values, interests, and goals. Be sure to use the Career Road Map at the end of the book to keep track of your answers. It will help you make choices when you reach the end of your journey.

Locate the Career Road Map at the end of the book!

Do You Have a Life Goal?

In addition to knowing yourself – your interests, values, preferences, and skills – it's important to start thinking about your life goals. Maybe you already have one, several, or maybe you have no idea what your life goals are. If you have no idea, it's important to begin to think about life goals, so that you can incorporate them in your career planning.

People choose what they want to be for many reasons. Be sure you have a reason for choosing your work– don't just take the easiest path. Many people don't find their ideal job because they haven't identified their life goals, let alone their interests, values, and skills. Think big to help you find your direction. Explore all possibilities and stay open-minded.

What Can a Life Goal Be?

Your life goal may involve being healthy, happy, and having enough money to travel the world. Your life goal may be to raise a large, happy family to nurture you in your old age. Your life goal may be to live your life in a quiet place, in a quiet way, by yourself.

When you choose your life goals, don't give up on your dreams, but remember that very few people can win a Nobel Prize or be President of the United States, so be honest and realistic when identifying life goals.

Write down a life goal:

_____

_____

_____

_____

_____

_____

Your life goal is just one piece of the puzzle. Knowing your life goal can help you make a crucial decision when choosing among jobs or careers.

Transfer this life goal to the Career Road Map at the end of the book.

2

Values Are Along for the Ride

"Meaning is not something you stumble across, like the answer to a riddle or the prize in a treasure hunt. Meaning is something you build into your own life."
– John W. Gardner, Founder of Common Cause and former Secretary of Health, Education, and Welfare

What are values? Values are the personal standards that are important to you. They are the things in life you care about most that form the basis for your life. Look back at the choices you've made in your life and think about how many times your values have driven your decisions. Did you take a job for a specific reason? Why did you choose a friend? Why did you end a friendship? The answers to these types of questions help you identify your values. Values give your life meaning.

Values are not easily left behind when you leave for work every day. They guide you at home and work, and everywhere in between. For example, perhaps you value helping others or having social status, or helping the environment or making money. In the workplace you may value working outdoors or in an unstructured indoor workplace, working as part of a team or working alone.

Values can and do change over your lifetime, so it's important to reassess your values from time to time. You should be able to clearly identify your values before you move on to making a career choice or a career change.

Identify Your Values

Let's identify your values now. The goal in this next section is to identify your **four** most important values.

What Do You Value the Most?

Read each value below and check the appropriate box to rate it
from 1 to 4 (1 = not important, 2 = rarely important, 3 = sometimes important, and 4 = very important).

	not important		very important	
My Environment	1	2	3	4
Job security (keep my job for a long time)				
Flexibility (choose how I perform my job responsibilities)				
Structured environment (do my work in a specific way at a specific time)				
Gives me time to spend with family/friends				
Quiet workplace				
Active, bustling workplace				
Public contact (interact with customers) Location of my choosing (work at home or office)				

	not important		very important	
	1	2	3	4
High salary/benefits				
Risk (potential to fail, but high rewards if I succeed)				
Flexible hours (choose the hours and days of the week or month I do my job)				
Low stress at work				
High stress job (lots of reward)				
Outdoor workplace (all or part of my day)				
Indoor workplace (all or part of my day)				
Diverse workplace (work with many types of people)				

Relationships

Leading and influencing others				
Working as part of a team				

	1	2	3	4
Working independently				
Having status with others				
Collaborating with others to make decisions				
Competitive workplace				
Non-competitive workplace				
Fun place to work				
Responsible for work of others				
High level of communication with others				
Feeling needed and appreciated by colleagues				
Loyalty (loyal to other workers and the employer)				
Honesty (honest workers and employer)				
Compassion (my co-workers and employer care about me)				

	not important		very important	
Work Content	1	2	3	4
Challenging work				
Help the environment				
Invent new things				
Creative work				
Work tasks change often				
Same work every day				
Physical challenge				
Help others				
Help the community				
Work with new technology				

	1	2	3	4

Learning opportunities (learn by doing)

Take initiative (action needed without direction from supervisor)

Advance my career (job leads to a higher level job)

Expertise (advanced knowledge needed to do the job)

Minimal knowledge needed to do the job

Make independent decisions

Next:

1. Look back at the choices marked highest (checkbox #4). Draw a star ☆ next to the 8 to 10 items you rated most important to you.

2. Circle your top four values from the starred items and write them below:

    1. _____   3. _____
    2. _____   4. _____

Add these four values to your Road Map at the end of the book, putting the most important value first.

Now that you have carefully chosen the values that are important to you, is there one value that you will never compromise? One that is so important that it must be in your job? If there is, write it in the box below:

Read the two case studies to see how values can affect your career choices:

Kayla's Dilemma

Right after college, Kayla was recruited for a very high paying job, working at home as a software game developer. One year later she felt frustrated and stressed out because she was working 50 hours a week in front of the computer. In high school she thrived on working as part of a team to create new computer software for a local elementary school. When she identified her values, she chose: Helping others, Flexible hours, Working as part of a team, and Helping the community. What went wrong with her job choice?

On the lines below, write down how Kayla's current job conflicts with her stated values.

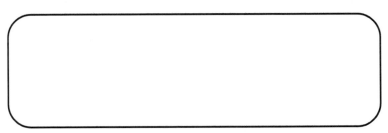

_____

_____

_____

_____

_____

_____

_____

Steve's Dilemma

Steve is an outstanding administrative assistant working for a very large chemical company. He recently earned his associate of arts degree. He thought the company he worked for would be a good fit because he is a very energetic person and wanted to work in a fast-paced, high paying business environment. All through high school he loved nature and spent most of his time outdoors with his friends. He was always a team player and got involved in community and environmental causes. During community college he enjoyed hiking, skiing, and cycling clubs. He joined the "Students for a Better Environment" and became president. Now he finds himself sitting alone in his cubicle 12 hours per day, only able to talk his colleagues on breaks, or by phone when his traveling boss calls in. He continuously struggles with his own beliefs and the impact his company has on the environment, even though he is not directly responsible. He has very little time for outdoor activities because of his long hours at work.

When he identified his values he chose: Active workplace, High salary/benefits, Time to spend with family and friends, Working as part of a team, and Help the environment.

On the lines below, indicate how Steve's current job conflicts with his identified values and past activities.

_____

_____
_____
_____
_____
_____
_____
_____
_____
_____

Your Most Important Value

Your values make you a unique individual. Always take your values into consideration as you make career choices. There may be a time when you will have to compromise on some of your most important values. It will be important to recognize the one value you have chosen not to compromise when making a career decision or applying for a future job.

Again, write that one value below:

3

Take a Road Trip

Most of us say, "I'm off to work now," but wouldn't it be great to
instead say "I'm off to do what interests me"
and then be paid for it?
— Reischman and Collard

People choose their careers for a variety of reasons. One of these reasons is the likelihood of working with people who share the same interests. John Holland, who created a career assessment called Self-Directed Search and the Holland Occupational Codes (see Chapter 10, Resources), has done extensive research on people who choose their careers based on their interests. His theory has been well documented and shows that people who are employed in the same types of work environments share many of the same interests. There is also a theory that says interest provides a stronger desire to learn a new skill. So, if you have a strong interest in something, it might take you less time to learn a new skill, than if you have no interest in it.

In fact, if you ask people around you why they chose the career they are in, you will find that they might answer like this... "Well, I was very interested in..." So, it's very important to take your interests into account as you choose your career.

The next exercise takes you behind the wheel for an imaginary cross-country road trip to explore your many interests.

My Interest Road Trip

There are six different road trips to choose from.

1. Read the statements under each trip.

2. Circle the symbol in front of each statement that interests you. (Think about people, places, and things you like to be around.)

3. Count the statements you circled and record the number in the box below each trip.

Trip #1 Interactors

🚌 You love the outdoors and the freedom to go where you choose. You spend hours redesigning and fixing up an old camper for your trip.

🚌 You drive up to the mountains for some great hiking and camping at a national park.

🚌 You meet an artist who sculpts from old metal and electrical parts. You love to work with your hands and ask to help. You weld metal and saw parts until it is finished.

🚌 Driving through a national forest, you stop at a small hotel overlooking a lake. The owners have an organic garden. You enthusiastically help them harvest the crop.

🚌 You take a helicopter ride over a huge waterfall, and land to explore the caverns behind it.

Number of items circled.

Trip #2 Researchers

? You read science travel magazines for your upcoming cross-country road trip. You enjoy spending hours on the Internet researching the places you want to visit.

? You have the opportunity to stop at an archeological site in the desert. You are thrilled when they ask you if you would like to help them collect and organize fossils.

? The next day you sail to an uncharted cave. You calculate the distance and risk to reach the cavern. You snorkel and then collect unusual rocks for later analysis.

? You camp under the stars with a telescope and talk about astronomy with friends.

? Your last stop is at a scientific laboratory. You are allowed to tour the lab and observe nationally recognized scientists conduct a gene slicing experiment.

☐ Number of items circled.

Trip #3 Creators

☀ After a long creative streak you decide to take a cross-country trip to re-energize and pick up some new and trendy ideas.

☀ You wrote a short piece for a publicity contest, and the sponsors asked you to write the program for a Broadway show. You're invited to attend the opening night and go backstage.

☀ You stop at an art gallery to see an exhibit and then go to a poetry club to listen to others.

☀ You like photography, so you decide to create a photographic journal of your trip.

☀ You meet a group of people who invite you to a week-long arts festival. You enjoy great music, art, and gourmet food with your new friends.

☐ Number of items circled.

Trip #4 Socializers

! You've gathered information from friends, chat rooms, and travel magazines. Much time and effort was put into having "people experiences" during your trip.

! You stop in a resort town where your friend's mother owns a small inn on the beach. You accept an invitation to stay a few days, and you socialize with all the guests at the inn.

! As it turns out, two people are heading the same way as you, so you decide to meet at a concert on the island for three days of music, fun, and camaraderie.

! At a rest stop you see a Houses for Humanity truck. The group tells you that two of their volunteers got sick, and they ask if you can help out for the day. You say yes.

! Childhood friends invite you to stop at their lake cabin for water sports and fun. When you arrive, there are already 20 people there and it's a huge party.

☐ Number of items circled.

Trip #5 Challengers

▸▸ You stop at the biggest canyon you've ever seen and see a trail. You buy water for your hike at a local store and unexpectedly take charge of a group that seems unsure of the terrain.

▸▸ You persuade two people you met from your hike to join you at your next stop. It's an entertainment awards show, where you're hoping to pick up some tickets.

▸▸ You take time for a little relaxation at a trendy beach resort where you meet a group of people who want you as their team captain for a relay contest. Full of energy, you accept.

▸▸ Your plan is to stop in the next city and see every sporting event you can in three days.

▸▸ The last town you stop in gives you an idea for a business that you'd like to explore. You stay a few days to observe and talk to people in town – as you're always looking for new ideas.

[   ] Number of items circled.

Trip #6 Organizers

⊟ You accept an offer to plan a group trip because you enjoy organizing and keeping track of things. You've made a complete schedule of all of your stops and activities for the trip.

⊟ You bring along lots of board games and stop at the beach the first night for game playing and camping under the stars.

⊟ Your favorite stop is a collector's paradise. Most people don't know about this museum where you can see hundreds of interesting and valuable collections.

⊟ You sign the group up for "The Festival of Innovation," a three-day outdoor event focused on how to do "anything" better.

⊟ You compile information from your cross-country trip and look forward to organizing useful tips on your website for future cross-country travelers.

[   ] Number of items circled.

Now look back at the three trips with the highest scores. These should be trips that you would most like to take. Think about why you chose those trips.

Record your road trip below and find out more about your interests on the next page.

 My Interest Road Trip

	Trip #
First choice (highest score):	_____
Second choice:	_____
Third choice:	_____

Interests and Work Environments

Trips #1 to #6 are listed below with descriptive words related to the trips.

1. In the list below, draw a star ☆ next to your top three trips.

2. Read the words under the chosen trips and circle the descriptive words and work environments that interest you.

Think about how your interests may factor into your career decisions.

____ **Trip #1 Interactors**

Athlete
Builder
Fixer
Mechanic
Technician
Outdoorsman/woman

Work environment:

Independent   Hands-on approach
Results-oriented   Sports-related
Physical   Interaction with environment
Practical   Work with things instead of ideas
Action-oriented

____ **Trip #2 Researchers**

Researcher
Investigator
Innovator
Inventor
Analyzer
Thinker

Work environment:

Independent   Technical
Curious   Flexible and unstructured
Problem-solving   Unconventional
Mathematical   Continuous learning
Project- and task-oriented Scientific

____ **Trip #3 Creators**

Innovator
Artist
Performer
Writer
Composer
Designer
Communicator

Work environment:

Independent   Variety
Expressive   Creative thinking
Non-conforming   Unstructured environment
Intuitive   Brainstorming opportunities
Imaginative

_____ **Trip #4 SOCIALIZERS**

Helper
Teacher
Communicator
Caretaker
Entertainer
Humanitarian
Facilitator
Team player
Good listener

Work environment:

Cooperative   Team-oriented
Friendly   Helping others
Interactive   Variety and action

_____ **Trip #5 Challengers**

Leader
Persuader
Adventurer
Risk-taker
Entrepreneur
Public speaker
Social organizer

Work environment:

Goal-oriented   Challenging
Flexible   Management opportunities
Independently owned business
Competitive/energetic environment

_____ **Trip #6 ORGANIZERS**

Administrator
Analyzer
Perfectionist
Collector
Planner
Organizer

Work environment:

Indoor office environment   Administrative opportunities
Detail-oriented workplace   Efficient/well-run workplace
Larger, structured workplace
Clearly defined work schedules and expectations

On your Road Map, write down the descriptive words you circled from the Interests and Work Environments section.

Side trip: If you would like to obtain a more in-depth interest profile, we suggest you take the Strong Interest Inventory or the Self-Directed Search (see Chapter 10, Resources).

4

Up the Mountain,
the Road to Success

When love and skill work together, expect a masterpiece!

— John Ruskin

Identify Your Skills

K nowledge of your skills is a very important part of developing a realistic and fulfilling career path. What you like to do can motivate you to learn and perfect certain skills. Since childhood you have been acquiring skills, and at each stage of your development they become more sophisticated.

For example, your high school teacher assigns a presentation that requires research, graphic design, and the use of multimedia tools. Ten years later you may have to give a presentation to the board of directors of a corporation using these same skills at an expert level.

As you plan your career, remember that there are always valuable skills to be learned no matter what you are participating in, whether it's volunteer work, sports, or caregiving. Skill building will enhance your options in the workplace at any stage in your life.

The workplace is changing rapidly and will continue to do so in the new millennium, so it is also important to understand your transferable skills. These are skills that provide you with the flexibility to work in many different settings. Transferable skills are often called "functional skills."

Transferable Skills: An Example

Jennifer likes to write, but doesn't know which direction she should choose to incorporate this skill into a future career. She realizes she has many job options, as shown in the diagram below. She can use her writing creatively, technically, in research, or in investigation. Her skill in writing is transferable to a variety of workplaces. Her next step should be to explore the different careers more thoroughly. Her final decision most likely will include other things she has learned about herself, such as her interests and values.

Jennifer's Career Options
Writing as a Transferable Skill

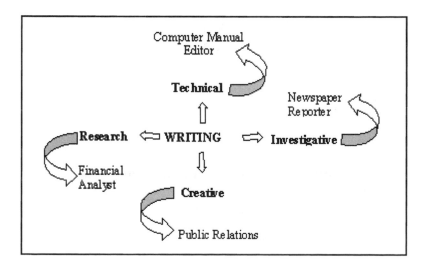

Skills and Ability

Skills are learned through knowledge and practice. Abilities are natural talents that a person has. Abilities generally affect how quickly a person will develop a skill.

The following Skill Card exercise will give you the opportunity to explore your skills. Building your skills is an ongoing process that will shift with changes in the workplace and your own personal preferences. The important thing to remember is that each skill becomes a building block to learning a new skill. When you have the opportunity to learn and use many of these skills, you will start to sort out which ones you really enjoy. If you choose a career that enables you to use the skills you enjoy, your job satisfaction will be enhanced.

Skills and Interests

The more interested you are in learning a new skill, the faster you will learn it. That is because interests generally motivate people to learn.

Transferable Skills and Technical Skills

The skills listed on the Skill Card exercise you are about to do are called "transferable" skills. These are skills that you can take with you from one work environment to another. They are your functional skills. Two examples of transferable skills are "teach" and "organize." Technical skills are those skills specific to the job. Examples would be operating a power saw or a microscope. Most people will have a combination of both transferable and technical skills. This combination provides flexibility and opportunities in many different fields. In general, people will have many more transferable skills than technical skills.

Keisha's Skills: An Example

Technical Skills	Transferable Skills
Bookkeeping	Problem-Solve/Prioritize
Ten-Key Operator	Write/Speak/Train

When you combine Transferable and Technical Skills you have a well-balanced skill profile.

 Create Your Skill Profile

Step #1   Cut out the skill cards located at the end of the book. Sort the cards into three sections—Base Skills, Midway Skills, and Summit Skills. It is <u>not necessary</u> to use all of the cards as you do this exercise.

Step #2   As you sort the cards, place (tape or clip) your Base Skills at the bottom of the mountain on pages 32-33. These are skills you perform well and like. (You are very comfortable and confident using these skills.)

Step #3   In the middle of the mountain, place your Midway Skills— skills you like or have, but could improve.

Step #4   Decide which skills you want to learn for your future career. Place these cards at the Summit (top).

Keep your cards sorted for this chapter.

Use the next two pages to sort your Skill Cards

GOING UP?
The Road to Success
(Sort your Skill Cards here)

Summit Skills: I would like to learn these skills for future careers.

Midway Skills: I have or like these skills, but they need improvement.

Base Skills:
I like these skills and perform them well.

The Beginning of My Journey
It doesn't matter how long it takes or how fast I take the curves,
as long as I never lose sight of the summit.

So that you may have a record of your skills, write your results down here.

Summit: Skills I would like to learn for my future career

Midway: Skills I have or like, and need to improve

Base: Skills I perform well and like (circle five strongest skills)

Keep your cards sorted for the next section!

Identify Skill Categories

Most work will require you to have more than one skill. Often these skills are related to each other in some way. As an example, *persuade*, *sell*, and *explain* fall into the same category of skills. The skill cards are automatically sorted into five categories. This will enable you to see your strengths in certain skill areas or categories.

Five Skill Categories: 1. Communication Skills
2. Organizational Skills 🗀
3. Design/Creative Skills 🖌
4. Problem-Solving Skills 💡
5. Leadership Skills 💼

Now look at the right-hand corner of each skill card for the symbol. In each section (Base, Midway, Summit), count the number of cards you have used with the same symbol. You will start to see patterns and strengths in certain skill areas. Record your results below:

Base Skills (skills I like and perform well)	# of Cards
Communication Skills ☎	
Organizational Skills 🗀	
Design/Creative Skills 🖌	
Problem-Solving Skills 💡	
Leadership Skills 💼	

Midway Skills (skills I like and need to improve)	# of Cards
Communication Skills ☎	
Organizational Skills 🗀	
Design/Creative Skills 🖌	
Problem-Solving Skills 💡	
Leadership Skills 💼	

Summit Skills (skills I would like to learn for my future career)	# of Cards
Communication Skills ☎	
Organizational Skills 🗁	
Design/Creative Skills 🎨	
Problem-Solving Skills 💡	
Leadership Skills 💼	

Strongest Skill Categories: Looking at your Base Skills, which two categories (of the five categories: Communication, Organizational, Design/Creative, Problem-Solving, Leadership) have the largest number of cards? These are your strongest.

Category: _____

Category: _____

Transferable Skills
These are skills that provide you with the flexibility to work in many different settings.

What skill categories can you use in many career settings?

_____

_____

_____

_____

Skills Example 1

Look at the following diagram. Do you think a lawyer would use the same skills in each of these work environments: International Law, Tax Planning, Corporate, City Planning, Judge, or Courtroom?

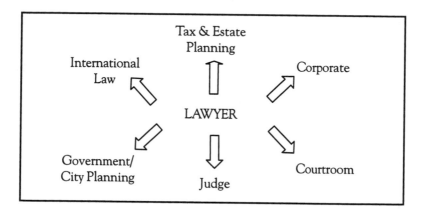

Which setting would emphasize speaking over writing?

_____

A lawyer can work in many different work settings, and a variety of skills may be needed. Remember that your skills may fit better in one setting, or that you may prefer one type of workplace to another.

Skills Example 2

The diagram below shows different workplaces for a teacher. Each setting may require different skills or use one skill more often.

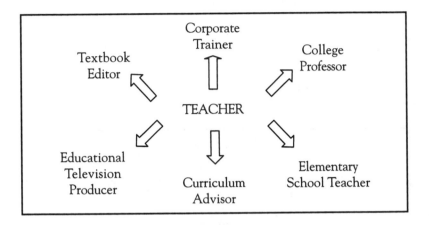

In what setting(s) would a teacher require more writing?

If you have previously explored certain career options, which top ten skills (include your strongest skills and need to learn) will be most needed for your future career(s)? If you have not yet explored careers that interest you, return to this section after Chapter 8.

In this chapter you have identified your top five skills and your two strongest skill categories. You've also identified the top ten skills (not skill categories) that you will need for a future career. Later in the chapter you will have the opportunity to set a goal to learn these new skills.

Record your top five skills and two top skill categories on your Road Map

Side trip: Once you begin to understand your interests and what skills you enjoy using, then it is time to explore different career options. The skill cards can also be used to research specific careers. After reviewing the cards, write down careers that use some of your skills. Do this by consulting O*NET, the *Occupational Outlook Handbook*, or the *Dictionary of Occupational Titles* (DOT), which list careers and skills needed (see Chapter 10, Resources).

5

What is Your
Navigation Style?

T he final area to explore is your navigation, or working, style. We all have a working style or preference for how we interact with others and how we interact in a job. It's not a personality trait, but a personal tendency. In a school setting, when you worked on group projects, you might have noticed that other students had different working styles than you. Teachers often assign group projects to give students an opportunity to experience working as a team.

Most teams have a mix of different styles. It's important to have work groups with different styles so that the group or team is efficient and effective. Employees that are flexible in their working style are more valuable to the company than those who cannot adapt their style.

Your working style should not help you pick a job, but help you determine "what kind" of employee you may be. It may also show that you have a preference for a particular career.

Working Styles Assessment

 Start by scoring each statement using this point system:

        1 = Least like me
        2 = Somewhat like me
        3 = Most like me

I.	Point
Like facts and numbers	
Perfectionist	
Logical, reasonable	
Good analyzer	
Do things step by step	
Total Points:	

II.	Point
Sociable	
People-oriented	
Talkative	
Team-oriented	
Friendly	
Total Points:	

III.	Point
Look at the big picture (see cause and effect, future impact of actions)	
Visual	
Idea person	
Creative	
Imaginative	
Total Points:	

Each of the boxes above indicates a working style. Here are the three working styles:

Section I – Analyzer or Detail-Oriented
Section II – People-Oriented
Section III – Creative

Your **highest** score indicates your working style. If two of your scores were high, you should indicate both working styles. Which category or categories did you score the highest?

_____

_____

Your score may have indicated that you were a people-oriented person, an analyzer, creative, or a combination of two or even three (if you scored equally in each category). If you scored over 12 or under 7 in any one category, you may want to work on one of the other categories to help you balance your working style. Being balanced or having strengths in two categories can help you be more adaptable in your work. It can also help you get the job of your choice, because more employers will want your skills.

Working Styles and Careers

You often find people with these working styles in this type of job:

Analyzer

Database Administrator	Paralegal
Veterinarian	Data Analyst
Computer Engineer	Budget Analyst
Financial Analyst	Archivist
Accountant	Archeologist
Biologist	Stock Broker
Auto Mechanic	Chief Financial Officer

People-Oriented

Social Worker

Counselor

Physical Therapist

Conservationist

Customer Service Representative

Hotel Manager

Human Resources Manager

Physician Assistant

Health Information Technician

Clergy

Education Administrator

Respiratory Therapist

Fundraiser

Public Relations Representative

Creative

Human Resources Manager

Desktop Publisher

Landscape Designer

Advertising Manager

Musician

Actor

Museum Curator

Interior Decorator

Public Relations Representative

Graphic Artist

Architect

Marketing Manager

Artist

Photographer

Set Designer

Video Producer

Chef

Determining your working style can help you choose a career field. Some jobs require people skills, some require a high level of analytical skills, and some require creativity. Most jobs can be a blend of different styles, but this depends on the work location, work content, and relationships needed to do the job.

Many people score high in two areas. You can use this to your advantage. Most jobs have elements of two or even three working styles within them. For example, a technical writer might need to be both analytical and creative in order to write technical, precise text in a creative and interesting manner. A construction worker might need to be people-oriented and analytical in order to both work well with a client and to measure precisely. In fact, creativity may be needed in order to design a job that meets the demands of a client. A choreographer must be extremely creative, but also people-oriented in order to direct a cast.

Here are some jobs that typically require more than one working style (depending on the description of the job):

People-Oriented and Creative

Publicist	Training Specialist
Photojournalist	Choreographer
Buyer	Public Relations Manager
Teacher	Food Service Worker
Construction	Occupational Therapist
Travel Agent	

People-Oriented and Analytical

Dentist	Optician
Nurse	Reporter
Journalist	Construction Worker
Dental Hygienist	Park Ranger
Sociologist	Computer Support Specialist
Police Officer	Physician
Lawyer	Emergency Medical Technician
	Bank Officer

Creative and Analytical

Writer	Animator
Architect	Scientist
Archeologist	Engineer

There are many more careers that combine various working styles. Some of the careers listed, depending on the type of job, could also fit under different working styles. You can add many more jobs to these lists by thinking about what skills are needed for each job.

On the Road Map, write down your top working style(s).

6

Need Directions?

The Changing World of Work

The world of work will change continuously throughout your life. Demographics, national and international events, information, technology, and science will influence careers in the 21st century. Because of this continuous change, it helps to know where you are coming from and where you are going. Having the skills to navigate in this changing world is crucial. It's important to map out your direction when you're planning a career.

There are always a few students in elementary school who know what they want to be when they grow up. They stay committed through high school, but even they may have to be flexible in our rapidly changing workplace. Companies will expect employees to be continuous learners and skill builders in this environment of flux. The technical skills you learned one month ago may be outdated six months from now. It is important to have more than one option when exploring a career choice. There are thousands of occupations to explore, and new jobs are being developed every year. As you look at your Road Map, you will start to see patterns. These patterns will help you to narrow down your options in order to conduct a more focused and successful career search.

Look for patterns!

✪✪✪✧✧✧✪✪✪✧✧✧✪✪✪

✪✪✪✧✧✧✪✪✪✧✧✧✪✪✪

Besides understanding your strengths in certain areas, it is also important to fulfill your needs. Having a job or career that is satisfying to you is important to your well being. Remember, you will spend a large portion of your life working. Why work in a job you don't enjoy?

Think about how many hours a day, a week, a year, and a lifetime you will spend working. Depending on where you live, type of commute, and the type of job you have (self-employed, union job, management, professional, or administrative position), your free time may be limited. It will be important to achieve a certain level of job satisfaction in order to be productive and enjoy your LIFE.

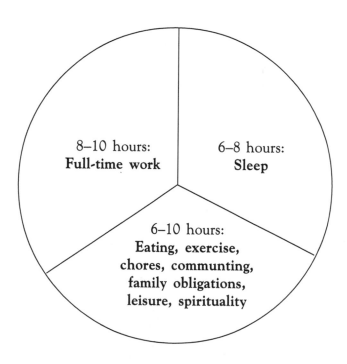

**There is not much time in a 24-hour day.
Be sure your work gives you satisfaction!**

Circumstance, Motivation, and Passion

This is all about empowerment—you have within you the power to shape your own destiny.
– Ron Krannich, author of "Change Your Job, Change Your Life"

Have you ever worked at a job that you really liked? Have you ever had a fabulous volunteer opportunity? Do you excel at a sport or hobby? Are there any other circumstances that play a role in your career choices?

Circumstance

There may have been a time in your life when things didn't go the way you would have liked, or an event took an unexpected turn that led you down an unplanned path. Unexpected circumstances have a way of popping up when you least expect them. The key to success is making these circumstances work for you. Seize the moment and think about positive outcomes and future opportunities.

For example: Your grandfather becomes ill and you need to postpone college and help out in his small coffee shop. What can you do during this time to advance your own career preferences?

- ❖ Explore night classes at the local college for transfer credit.
- ❖ Network with your customers about careers.
- ❖ Visit the Chamber of Commerce to learn more about other businesses in your area.
- ❖ Volunteer (find your passion).

Another example: You have a part-time job at a department store. Your manager guarantees you a promotion and asks you to stay on full time after you graduate from high school. This is not what you want to do for the rest of your life, but it sounds great for right now. What are your options?

* ❖ Continue to explore other career and educational options.
* ❖ Learn as much as you can on the job.
* ❖ Set short-term and long-term goals.

Is there a circumstance that could affect your career choice (such as a personal or family crisis, an unexpected encounter or experience, an unforeseen opportunity)?

_____

_____

Motivation

What motivates you? Your personal motivation will help you achieve your goals and succeed in choosing a career path. It is important to know what makes you want to do your best.

> # Motivation = Success

 As you continue on your road to success, circle the following words that motivate you to do your best work (choose all that apply):

I am motivated to do my best when I have:

Respect   Challenge   Recognition   Job pressure

Approval   Satisfaction   Job security   Interest

Reward	Curiosity	Money	Passion
Pride in my work	Power	Parental pressure	Advancement opportunity

 Write down what motivates you:

_____

_____

_____

_____

_____

_____

Add this to your Road Map.

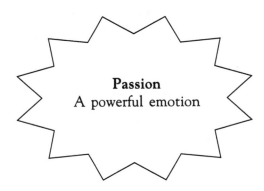

Passion
A powerful emotion

Passion

To determine what type of work will give you a sense of satisfaction at the end of the day and one that you will be happy with at the end of the year, it's important to find work that fills you with passion. Are you passionate about something in your life now?

Think about things in your life that you love doing. It could be a hobby, a sport, a school subject that you really enjoy, a particular skill that you have, or a place that you love.

What are your passion(s)?

_____

_____

As you read this chapter, think about ways to incorporate passion into a career plan. Keep in mind that what you may be passionate about today may change as you grow older.

Add this to your Road Map.

Here are some job examples based on passion:

Photography (hobby)	
Commercial Photographer	Gallery Owner
Portrait Photographer	Medical Photographer
Graphic/Animation Designer	Layout Designer
Corporate Historian	Art Consultant
Advertising Assistant	Museum Curator

Sports
(team and individual activity)

Sports Photographer	Sports Announcer
Sports Scout	Athletic Trainer
Recreation Director	Promotional Event Planner
Sports Agent	Sports Psychologist
Sports Therapist	Sporting Company Salesperson

Computer Games
(leisure activity)

Software Designer/Tester	Software Engineer
Stage Technician	Toy Maker
Computer Animator	Graphic Design Engineer
Quality Engineer	Software Sales Representative

English
(school subject)

Journalist	Teacher/Professor
Television Producer	Technical Writer
Editor	Public Relations Director
Novelist/Poet	Lawyer
Communications Director	Broadcaster

Identifying Career Options: Road Map Review

It's important to review your Road Map as you work your way through this book. Before you start, read Alberto's Road Map to see what his next steps will be.

Alberto's Road Map

Life Goal	Freedom to work independently and be challenged
Values	Location of my choosing, creative work, help the community, challenging work
Interests/ Environments	Socializer, challenger, teacher/ interactive, variety
Skill Categories	Communication, Design/ Creative
Working Style	Creative
Circumstance	Hired by a small independent newspaper as a summer intern to critique local restaurants and write a weekly column. Worked for a local caterer on Saturday nights.
Motivation	Satisfaction, challenge
Passion	Love to cook

Alberto's next step would be to take all of this information, and see if there is a pattern. He noticed that he wanted challenging and creative work, a career involving food, working with people, and being independent. He chose to look in the *Dictionary of Occupational Titles* (DOT) and *O*NET* for careers with that focus. He read *Culinary Arts and Career Starter* (by Mary Masi, Learning Express, 1999). He also researched sites on the Internet: foodindustryjobs.com, cooljobs.com, and culinary.com.

Here are the career options he chose: Chef, caterer, nutritionist, food taster, restaurateur, cooking school instructor, food critic, cookbook designer.

Alberto, we know you love to cook, but please bring a bag lunch to school!

Identify Career Options

Now it's your turn. Start by looking at your Career Road Map, review each section, and look for logical patterns. Think about jobs that would be an ideal fit for your values, skills, and working styles. What job options or potential careers would fit your profile? What interests you the most? Are there skills or knowledge that you need to gain before you can pursue your desired career? What are you passionate about?

How do you find patterns on your Road Map? Look for words and phrases that go together, complement each other, or even overlap. For example, you notice that you are people-oriented (your working style), a socializer (your interest), and like working as part of a team (your value). You would write this down on the lines below. If you have difficulty, ask someone close to you to review your profile and give you suggestions for jobs or careers. You could ask a parent, a friend, or someone you work with. If you wish, a career counselor can help you analyze the information. Career counselors can be found at any of the career centers across the country (see Chapter 8).

My Patterns

_____

_____

_____

_____

Next, spend some time researching and exploring your career options. Your research should include:

❖ Exploring *Occupational Outlook Handbook, Dictionary of Occupational Titles* (DOT), or O*NET
❖ Reading books and magazine articles
❖ Volunteering at conventions of interest
❖ Reading association newsletters
❖ Conducting informational interviews (see chapter 9)
❖ Using the Internet (see chapter 10)
❖ Researching programs at colleges and universities
❖ Looking up salary ranges on the Internet

The O*NET is an excellent resource for exploring careers. You can also use the Internet as an exploration tool. For example, if you want to find out more information about sports agents, use an Internet search engine to look for key words such as sports agent job, sports agent salary, or sports agent career; or look for books such as *50 Cool Jobs in Sports* or *Career Opportunities in the Sports Industries*.

Now choose three careers or occupations that fit your profile. Remember that these careers are simply several options for you. At some point you will need to use your decision-making skills to make a choice, but until that time comes, you should focus on exploring career possibilities.

List your top career options here:

_____

_____

_____

Add these to your Road Map.

Is It a Match?

When you put your Road Map profile side by side with the careers you gathered, in some cases they will match very neatly and in others they will not. It is important to recognize when a choice is not a good fit. For example, you may think you want to be a nurse, but you've discovered that you are not people-oriented and you don't like science. In this case, a career in nursing may not be in your best interest. Be sure to take careers off your list that do not mesh with your profile. Expand your career search if necessary.

And If All Else Fails...

Life will not always be predictable, and sometimes the best plan will not take shape easily. Circumstance or serendipitous experiences may determine your career choice. Embrace circumstance as a reason to seize an opportunity. A mentor may come into your life at a time when you are making a career decision, or you might unexpectedly meet someone who works in a field that fascinates you, or you may face a personal setback that will change your plans. Whatever the reason, recognize these as learning experiences. There will be many forks in the road along your career path. No matter which way you choose to go, remember to use your career self-management skills with the Career Road Map to help you reach your destination.

> *My career had all the straight-line consistency of a tangled ball of yarn. Did I know where I was headed? Absolutely not! Did I plan my career moves in a logical progression? Absolutely not. There was no grand design. I was a California boy, stumbling cheerfully through life, succeeding, falling on my face, picking myself up and plunging ahead, holding onto some simple values, trying to live with a civil heart as someone said, always learning, always trying, always wondering.*
>
> – John W. Gardner, Founder of Common Cause; former Secretary of Health, Education, and Welfare

7

A Fork in the Road, Choosing a Direction

When you come to a fork in the road, take it!

– Yogi Berra

By now you've spent some time assessing your skills, interests, preferences, and values, and even chosen some career options. Your Road Map contains an abundance of information that can help you choose a career and get you started setting short- and long-term goals. It's important to establish goals so that you know where you are going and how to get there. Studies have repeatedly shown that individuals who verbally communicate goals to others are more likely to achieve their goals. Those who also write down their goals are even more successful in achieving them.

What if I still don't know what I want to do?

Gather enough information on yourself and your options to make an informed decision about *possible* jobs or careers. Ask a parent, counselor, or friend to give you another perspective on yourself and your possible options. Find just one place to start and go from there.

What if I have too many choices?

Decision-making is a part of the career planning process. This may mean narrowing down the choices, choosing the right goals, and/or choosing the right direction with regard to career and educational options. It means choosing a direction when there is a fork in the road. Up until now, you've spent most of your time exploring your options. You may ask yourself, *"What happens if I don't make the right decision?"*

And then ask:

"What is the worst thing that can happen if I make the wrong decision?"

If you can live with the outcome, then you can face the fear of making the wrong decision. Most people who make the wrong career decision will generally say that it may have been the wrong decision, but it was an important learning experience. Sometimes the wrong decisions also lead us to alternative careers that weren't considered before.

Here's how to make a good career decision:

1. **Use Information:** Gather all of the information you can before making a decision.

2. **Be Realistic:** Will it really work for you?

3. **Be Balanced:** Be practical, as well as creative in your thinking

4. **Be Flexible:** Leave some room for flexibility in your decision-making process. Have other options.

Use the worksheet below to help you make a decision on your career options.

Steps for Making Good Decisions

1. I would like to make a decision regarding the following:

2. I have gathered information from the following sources:

a.

b.

c.

3. Jot down the positive things that could happen (Pro) and the negative aspects (Con) of your decision:

      Pro   Con

4. What are my other options?

5. Evaluate your pros, cons, and other options to help you make your decision. Ask for help from others if necessary.

What is a goal?

A goal is a statement of intention. Studies have repeatedly shown that those individuals who verbally communicate goals to others are more likely to achieve these goals. Those who also write down their goals are even more successful in achieving the goals.

Set Your Goals

It's time to set your goals. Think about three things you need to do to pursue your desired career, or just to get started moving in that direction. The items you choose may be related to the education you need for the job, further exploration of potential careers or jobs, interviewing those with a position you seek, or even getting a summer job in the desired field.

What are the three things you need to do to get started pursuing your desired career?

1. _____

2. _____

3. _____

Goal setting is a flexible process: Goals are meant to change as you grow and change. Many people shy away from setting goals because they have not had success in achieving their goals. Remember to be realistic in setting goals for yourself. Ask yourself how motivated you were to actually achieve a desired goal in the past. The success in goal setting depends on your honest assessment and realistic expectations in making the goal come true.

Henry Ford once said, *"Obstacles are those frightful things you see when you take your eyes off your goal."*

Why should you set goals?

Setting goals enables you to take action. It motivates you to focus on what you want and how to get there. Many times there are so many possibilities that it's hard to sort out what you really want. Setting a goal, even a small one, will help you take steps towards a realistic and meaningful career.

Keep the following points in mind as you fill in the Goal Setting Worksheet at the end of the chapter:

❖ Set realistic goals with realistic time frames.

❖ Create long-term goals, short-term goals, and action steps.

❖ For each long-term goal, make a list of all of the tasks that you should do to achieve the goal. These tasks should be listed as short-term goals or action steps.

❖ Set aside and schedule the time to accomplish your tasks.

❖ Solicit support from others in reaching your goals.

❖ Reward yourself for accomplishments. Acknowledge all steps, no matter how small.

Road Map Review

Let's review Matt's Road Map. What will his next steps will be?

Matt's Road Map

Life Goals	To be happy, travel, and have enough money to live comfortably
Values	Flexibility, challenging work, creative work, fun place to work
Interests/Work Environments	Athletic, creative, organizer, independent, results-oriented, communicator
Skill Categories	Communication skills, organizational skills
Working Style	Creative and people-oriented
Motivation	Independence, interest, money
Passion	Photography, video editing, hockey
Career Options	Photojournalism or video production, human resources, marketing

Next, Matt explored his career interests, comparing what types of skills, work environments, and values were needed for each career, and then validated this with his life goals. He researched college programs in each area and made an appointment with someone who worked in each field, asking them about their job. He decided that video production would give him the most satisfaction.

He then formulated a long-term goal: Get a college degree in video production by 2006.

He also made plans for two short-term goals:

1. Obtain a summer job at a video production company.

2. Apply to a college offering a video production degree in the fall.

 Take a few minutes to review your Road Map. Identify at least one long-term goal to use in the next section. Your long-term goals should have something to do with your career destination.

It's your turn to set some goals!

Goal-Setting Worksheet

 Choose one career goal. Decide whether it is a **Long-Term Goal**, a **Short-Term Goal**, or an **Action Step**. Enter goals and action steps in the appropriate boxes.

Long-Term Goals (2–10 years)—General statements describing your career destination

Short-Term Goals (6 months–1 year)—Specific actions leading to your long-term goals

Action Steps (1 month)—Very specific behaviors leading toward your short-term goals

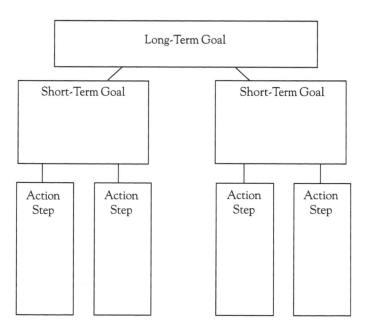

You can also write your goals this way.

Malika's goals:

Long-Term Goal: To get my college degree in computer science by June 2005.

Short-Term Goals:

1) Get college catalog and application for enrollment:

2) Meet with counselor to check requirements for degree and what classes I'll need to take:

3) Seek financial aid:

Action Steps for each of the Short-Term Goals:

1) Get college catalog and application for enrollment:

- ❖ call undergraduate admissions to request application

- ❖ schedule time next Wednesday evening to fill out application

2) Meet with counselor to check requirements for degree and what classes I'll need to take:

- ❖ call undergraduate admissions to request transcripts

- ❖ call counseling office to set up appointment for three weeks from today

3) Seek financial aid:

- ❖ call the financial aid office to request information

- ❖ schedule a trip to the library to research grants, loans, and other forms of financial assistance

---

List your long-term and short-term goals on the Career

Road Map at the end of the book.

Congratulations! You have almost completed the book. Now that you know more about where you're going, spend some time considering how to get there. The next few chapters focus on gathering more information about your career options to help you land the job of your dreams or start training for your future career. Chapter 8 will help you reach your career destination by teaching you how to conduct informational interviews to explore the careers that interest you the most. This chapter also examines the importance of listening to others to learn more about yourself and your career choices. Chapter 9 provides you with tools to get the job you most desire—how to write resumes, cover letters, and interview for a job.

Review your Road Map again and take action now by pursuing the goals you have listed on the previous pages.

Using Your Road Map in the Future

Now that you know how to put together a Career Road Map, you can use these career self-management tools throughout your life. Refer back to your Road Map often to reassess or reaffirm your skills, values, interests, and goals. Don't forget that your passion is also important! Remember, when you reach a fork in the road you will need to make a decision on which way to go. The good news is that there is really no wrong way because there is no final destination. This is just one of many road trips you will have in your life, but now you know how to create a map that will guide you to your ideal career.

8

Fuel for Thought: Listening

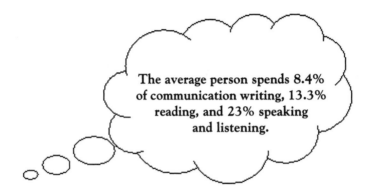

The average person spends 8.4% of communication writing, 13.3% reading, and 23% speaking and listening.

Listen for Success

Listening can effectively help you in all aspects of your life, and it is extremely important in the workplace today.

Our country has shifted from manufacturing as our primary business to providing knowledge and services to people around the globe.

How work has changed through the past century:

The Industrial Age ⟶ Service/Information Providers

Think about what this means. For a company or organization to be successful in providing services to people, it has to

❖ listen to what people want
❖ fulfill their needs
❖ supply ongoing support

As one individual in this big picture, you can be successful in your career if you use these tips when listening:

❖ be an active listener (focus on every word using verbal and nonverbal cues as appropriate)

❖ be nonjudgmental

❖ refrain from interrupting the speaker

❖ focus on the communication style of others (verbal and nonverbal) by adapting your own style

❖ listen to find solutions

Reaching your destination through better listening

Choosing a career requires lots of time and energy. If you are a good listener, you can use your time wisely and obtain knowledge that you will never find in any career book. Listening carefully is important for informational interviews as well as job interviews. During an informational interview, become a career detective and listen to what people tell you about their career paths. Most people love to talk about themselves, so it's usually very easy to obtain information about their jobs. Listen for positive and negative comments and assess their importance in relation to your career goals. What may be a negative for one person in his or her job may be a positive for you.

Listening: The Value of Informational Interviews

Information is the key to success. Whether you're writing a research paper or planning your own future, the more information you obtain, the better the outcome. The most honest and informative information on careers generally comes from people in the workplace.

The purpose of the informational interview is to provide you with the opportunity to obtain information that you need in order to choose the right career direction. **An informational interview is not a job interview.** However, it is a great opportunity to access a work environment you are interested in and practice your communication skills. **You** are the interviewer! Informational interviews are helpful in the following ways:

- ❖ Meet people with experience in a career field.

- ❖ Learn what skills and education you may need to be successful.

- ❖ Observe the work environment.

- ❖ Receive feedback on your career plan.

- ❖ Develop your interviewing skills.

- ❖ Determine if your career choice is realistic and obtainable.

Practicing for an informational interview

An informational interview provides a wonderful opportunity to practice your listening skills. Before you schedule an informational interview, practice with people you know.

- ❖ When practicing, maintain eye contact and focus on the individual.

- ❖ Do not write anything down during the practice interview.

- ❖ After the person responds, write down the information you were given and have him or her review your notes for accuracy.

When it's time for a real informational interview, you will have practiced your listening skills and gained valuable experience. Read on about how to set up an informational interview.

Arranging the informational interview:

First choose the career field or company that interests you. If you don't know where to begin, a good place to start is your local business Yellow Pages available from the phone company. Start browsing and mark with a highlighter companies that look interesting. If you are reluctant to call for an interview, you may introduce yourself by letter first, stating that you will followup with a phone call.

Make a list of people whom you know: parents, friends, teachers, counselors, and relatives. Many of these people will be able to provide you with referrals. Ask them, *"Who might it be helpful to talk to?"* There may be opportunities at your school through "Job Shadow Programs" to conduct an informational interview. Lastly, the Internet enables you to access associations, conventions, and career networks and organizations. Many times conventions will need local volunteers.

You may have an unplanned opportunity to conduct an informational interview on an airplane, standing in line at a movie, or at a department store counter. Wherever and whenever you conduct your informational interview, follow these six guidelines to ensure success.

1. Scheduling the interview

Informational interviews are short meetings (30 minutes maximum) at a mutually agreed upon time. It is to your advantage to schedule the meeting at the person's place of employment. Introduce yourself as someone wanting guidance because you are interested in that career. It is usually easier to arrange an interview when you have a referral. Be aware that many people have busy schedules, so calling or e-mailing to schedule an interview on a Monday morning may not be a good idea! Most people will be happy to discuss their career path, but if you do not get a response, it usually means the person you contacted is just too busy.

2. Preparing for the interview

It is important that you prepare ahead of time. Know something about the person's career field and company. Information can be obtained from the human resources department, your local public library, and sometimes on the Internet. Prepare a list of questions that are important to you. Here are some sample questions:

> Tell me about your career path.
>
> Did you plan to have this career?
>
> How do you spend a typical day?
>
> What types of people do you work with?
>
> What do you like or dislike about your job?
>
> What type of education do you need for your position?
>
> What are the top five skills you need in this career?
>
> What part of your job is the most challenging?
>
> Can you advance from this job? In this career?
>
> What is the salary range?
>
> Do you see your field changing in the future?
>
> Do you think your job will still be here in 20 years?
>
> What career planning suggestions do you have for me?
>
> Do you have any other suggestions to help me obtain more information?
>
> Could you refer me to someone else in your field?

3. Beginning the interview

Remember to arrive at least 10 minutes early for your interview. Relax and observe your surroundings. Dress the same way you would dress for a job interview. Shake hands and thank him/her for taking the time to meet with you. Smile and try to be enthusiastic. As you ask questions, try to maintain eye contact as much as possible while jotting down notes.

4. Gaining information from the interview

Your initial question should be one that helps you get to know the person. You may want to choose *"Tell me about your career background"* or *"Tell me about your career path"* as your first question. Make sure you allow the person you are interviewing be the expert. You are there to listen and learn. Remember to ask your most important questions first, since you have a limited amount of time.

5. Concluding the interview

At the end of the interview it is appropriate to ask for additional names of people who may be able to help you. If the person you just interviewed doesn't have the type of job you're interested in, he/she may know someone who has a job more in line with your career goal. Make sure to thank your interviewee sincerely for his or her time and guidance. Before you leave, ask for a business card, so you have the correct spelling and address for a thank-you note.

6. After the interview

The thank-you letter should be sent within the first few days after your interview. Here's a sample thank-you note to get you started.

Date:

Person's Name:
Title:
Company Name:
Address:

Dear Mr./Ms._____,

Thank you for _____(time, valuable information, clarification, encouragement, guidance and thoughtfulness). I was really impressed by _____ (mention something that stood out for you during the interview).

I will let you know what my future plans are. (Drop him/her a quick note when you go to school or get your first job.)

> Thank you for _____ (any names this person gave you and when you will contact them). I plan to _____(what will you do next?)
>
>
> Sincerely,
>
>
> Your Name

You have just gained first-hand information about your career. Use this information to help you make a decision about pursuing that particular field or company. What were the top five skills needed for his or her job? Compare these with the skills you listed on your Road Map. Is this the type of workplace that suits you? What else might you need to get started in this field? Do you need specific training or should you major in a specific area?

Listening: Interviewing for a Job

Most people who interview for a job think that the interview is one-sided and that the employer is the one who does all of the listening. False! Actually, it's even more important that you, the job candidate, hear what the employer is saying. You'll learn more about job interviews in Chapter 9, but remember that listening is important in all interviews. When you are ready, practice a job interview with a friend or family member, keeping the following listening points in mind:

- ❖ **LISTEN** to assess communication style (the person hiring you is soft-spoken or gregarious, confident or unsure of himself, formal or informal, knowledgeable or not).

- ❖ **LISTEN** to the kinds of questions you're being asked.

- ❖ **LISTEN** to the question carefully, so you can answer with specific examples.

❖ **LISTEN** for comments that let you assess the culture (what people seem to have in common in the workplace).

❖ **LISTEN** for negative comments about the work or people.

❖ **LISTEN** to how people interact with each other.

❖ **LISTEN** to find out if this is the job you really want.

Interviewing is a give-and-take process. Both you and the potential employer need to listen carefully. The better you listen, the better the outcome. **Remember, listening is a KEY factor in all interviews.**

Successful interviewing is not as complicated as hundreds of books make it seem. You can go to the library and bookstores and look up scores of potential questions employers may ask you. It will be worth your time to only practice answering general questions. Knowing the answer to all the questions only helps if the employer asks that particular question! Listening carefully is just as important.

In general, 80 percent of the interviews conducted have had a least one question answered by a candidate incorrectly, partially answered, or repeated for the candidate. This happens all the time. So, if you listen well in an interview, you will be better equipped to answer the question and stand out as an excellent communicator.

Becoming a better listener will not only help you in job interviews, but also on the job and in life.

Listen to Yourself and Others

It's important to listen to others to gain a new perspective on your career potential. Studies have shown that many people look to their parents or people who have raised them for career guidance. After all, these are the people that you spent your formative years with and know you best. They may be able to tell you what you're good at, but, as you learned in Chapter 4, you may be good at something, but not really like it. How do you listen to others? How do you listen to yourself?

 First, ask people who know you well to share information about you. Ask them these questions:

- How would you describe me?
- What are my strengths? What are my weaknesses?
- What do you think I'd be good at doing?
- Where do you see me in 10 years?

Write down what they said:

_____

_____

_____

_____

_____

_____

_____

After they provide all of this wonderful information, write them a quick note of thanks. Here's an example to get you started.

Dear _____,

I'm embarking on a career life journey that I hope will enable me to find the career of my dreams. Please be patient with me and support me on my road to self-discovery and happiness. It may or may not be the shortest and most direct path to success, but I need to chart my own course to attain my dream job.

I appreciate your advice and guidance. Thank you for telling me what you think I'm good at and trusting me to know myself. Please continue to listen when I share my ideas with you. I am a unique individual with my own career plan. When I compile my values, interests, skills, style, motivation, and, most of all, my passion, I will see where it leads me. As

> I learn life-long career self-management skills, your support on my jour-
> ney is greatly appreciated.
>
> Sincerely,
> Your Name

What this all means is that you know yourself better than anyone else, but it sometimes helps to get feedback on how others perceive you, so that you have more information to work with.

Remember: Information is the most powerful thing you can have!

What we have to learn to do, we learn by doing.

– Aristotle

Support of a Mentor

Key Point ⌐

Studies have shown that being mentored is directly linked with academic and professional success.

Why find a mentor?

There are many reasons to seek out a mentor. The most compelling reason is that it's extremely helpful to have someone who knows you and believes in you, who can guide you in your learning. Mentors provide an opportunity for you to learn new skills and gain access to people and workplaces that would otherwise take years to find. You can obtain insight from an experienced individual who shares your passion, and who can advise and encourage you when you have to make career choices or life decisions.

Whom should you choose for a mentor?

Sometimes mentors are right under your nose and you don't realize it. In Gordan F. Shea's book, *Mentoring* (AMA Publications, 1994), he writes:

Mentors come in all styles and types. They may be patient listeners who permit us to ventilate strong feelings (anger, fear or grief) that are keeping us stuck in place; they may be stern taskmasters who hold us to the highest standards of performance we are capable of (even when we don't think we are capable of them); they may be patient encouragers who help us move toward some goal of our own. Or, they may be technical or professional people who teach us the ropes, drawing out skills we didn't know we had (or we vaguely recognized) and lighting a spark within us.

Think of people in your life who would make good mentors.

- Teachers
- Coaches
- Employers
- Friends
- Counselors
- Club organizers
- Community officials
- Local chamber of commerce members

Contact one of these potential mentors and establish a relationship.

Write your potential mentor's name here:

Where else can you find a mentor?

There are many ways to find a mentor. If you are currently in high school or college, you have the opportunity to join clubs, take part in events, participate in job shadow programs, and work part time. These are all good places to look for a mentor.

There are also national programs such as Junior Achievement International, Mentoring USA, and The National Mentoring Program. Many states and cities have their own programs that can be located on the Internet or the business Yellow Pages of the phone book.

Using a Career Counselor

This book promotes career self-management. It is the navigation system to point you in the right direction, re-route you if you get lost along the way, and support and encourage you as the front seat passenger on your career road trip.

If you are currently in high school or college, take advantage of your career center. This center will help you explore and get to know yourself better at important crossroads in your life. Most career centers have how-to books and publications, video and audio recordings, job information, counseling, classes, assessments, and testing.

If you are no longer in school, there are community career centers, community college career centers, private centers and career counselors in private practice. Here are some guidelines for choosing a career counselor:

- ❖ Always ask to see a person's credentials.

- ❖ Find another counselor if he or she seems overly concerned about fees.

- ❖ Do not sign any up-front contracts.

- ❖ Be concerned if you are bombarded by requests for costly testing.

- ❖ Ask yourself if you communicate well with the counselor. (Is he or she a good listener?)

- ❖ Be sure you understand what the counselor has to offer you (i.e., resume writing or counseling).

During your counseling session, remember that:

❖ Testing (assessments) can be useful to initiate a valuable discussion with a career counselor, but it's up to you to provide as much information as you can about yourself in order to achieve your goal.

❖ Sometimes, just hearing it from others is validation that you are on the right track and that's what you needed the most (the "Aha, I knew that all along!" theory).

Listening is an important part of the career self-management process. Listen to others, but also remember to listen to yourself. You know yourself best, so don't be pushed into a career that you don't really like (but were afraid to say). Keep all comments and feedback in perspective. Good luck!

 Review your short- and long-term goals. Add another goal, if necessary. For example, you may want to find a mentor, consult a career counselor, or set up an informational interview.

9

Reaching Your Destination

Write Your First Resume and Cover Letter

There are hundreds of books available on how to write resumes and cover letters. Be sure to look at different examples before you write your own.

The purpose of a resume is to get you an interview. The resume is the first impression an employer will have of you, so it is important to present yourself in a way that will make the employer want to talk to you in person.

When you begin to write your resume, use the following guidelines:

1. Your first resume should be on one page.
2. Use good quality white or light-colored paper with matching envelopes.
3. Place your name at the top of the page.
4. Describe your experience with specific skills, accomplishments, and education.
5. Lay out your resume so it is easy to read (no columns, italics, shadows, etc.).
6. Check spelling and punctuation carefully.
7. Have at least two people proofread it.

8. Use standard fonts.

9. Do not use a font size below 10.

Most large companies and organizations will scan your resume and place it in their computer database. A smaller company or organization will ask the hiring manager to read your resume. Regardless of whether a computer or a person first reads your resume, you will need to write it a similar way.

Accomplishment Statements

It's important to have accomplishment statements prepared for use in your resume and cover letter. An accomplishment statement is a detailed statement that lets the employer know what you've achieved in the past. These statements typically showcase your strong skills or values. The statements you use do not have to be work-experience related. They can include volunteer work, school-related projects, applicable hobbies, and family experiences. Before you write your resume, spend some time writing accomplishment statements that are relevant to the job.

The following are action-oriented words to help you write accomplishment statements. They are used at the beginning of the statement:

Arranged	Evaluated	Presented
Calculated	Helped	Prioritized
Collected	Implemented	Produced
Computed	Installed	Programmed
Constructed	Led	Researched
Coordinated	Managed	Scheduled
Created	Motivated	Sold
Decided	Operated	Surveyed
Designed	Organized	Trained
Developed	Planned	Wrote

Here are examples of accomplishment statements:

Skill: WRITE
Accomplishment Statement: Wrote proposal for freshman sports program at my high school.

Skill: ORGANIZE
Accomplishment Statement: Organized 200 students to sign a petition for freshman sports at my high school.

Skill: PERSUADE
Accomplishment Statement: Persuaded school administrators to reinstate freshman sports at my high school.

When you're ready to write your resume, you may want to combine your accomplishment statements as shown below:

Skills: WRITE, ORGANIZE, PERSUADE
Accomplishment Statement: *Wrote* proposal and *organized* 200 students to *persuade* the administration that freshman sports were a critical and important part of our school. The administration reinstated the program.

Your accomplishment statements will help you write your resume!

Tip: Keep a computer file of your accomplishment statements and update every six months.

From your Road Map or Chapter 4, write down two of your strongest skills:

1. _____

2. _____

On the lines below, write your accomplishment statement for each skill. Be sure to start with an action-oriented word:

1. _____
   _____
   _____
   _____
   _____

2. _____
   _____
   _____
   _____
   _____

Now try combining two skills:

_____
_____
_____
_____
_____

Now that you have some accomplishment statements, use them when writing your resume. Be sure that the accomplishment statements reflect what the employer is looking for.

More Tips for Writing Resumes

❖ Be honest! (People have ruined their careers by embellishing a resume.)

❖ Stay away from using words ending in –ing (use scheduled instead of scheduling).

❖ Use results-oriented statements such as *"because of my design.... the school was able to..."*

❖ Research the job you are applying for and use industry language on your resume.

❖ Do not include personal information on a resume such as age, ethnicity, or marital status.

The Resume Outline

There are two types of resumes. A chronological resume states experience in chronological order. This is the type of resume you will see most often and the one covered in this chapter. The other type of resume is a functional resume. This type emphasizes skill categories. It is commonly used when a person wants to change his/her career direction, re-enter the workplace, or go back to school.

How to Write a Chronological Resume for the Young Adult

Here's an outline to help you write a resume:

Personal Information:

> Name, Address, Phone (including area code), Email

Objective:

> State your employment goal. This is an optional category. Remember to change your objective each time you apply for a job. Be specific. For example, *To obtain a position as a lifeguard at a summer camp for disabled children.*

Strengths:

> Examples of headings you can use: Accomplishments, Summary of Qualifications, or Summary of Skills. Your list should reflect what the employer is looking for. It should highlight your strengths. For example, if you are applying for a summer camp job: *Four years of leadership and peer counselor training in high school.*

Education:

Begin with your highest degree and work backward—from college to high school. List academic honors if relevant.

Experience:

First, give the dates of employment, job title, place of employment, city, state. Then, list accomplishment statements. Use your action words and results-oriented statements to describe your experience. Emphasize your strongest skills first. Try to directly relate your experience to the job you are applying for, using specific details. For example, *Organized and trained twenty students for an extremely successful drug awareness program. Eight-hour program reached 1,200 public school students. Wrote evaluation form and presented results at school board meeting.* Include volunteer experience if relevant.

Additional Information or Training:

Community involvement or other training such as volunteer work, relevant hobbies, honors, awards, athletics, talents, languages spoken. If there is information that doesn't fit under experience, then you will need to create a category for relevant information

Here's an example of a resume for a young adult with work experience:

26 Planet Road
Zicon, CA 78654
(769) 675-5888
kmatthews@zol.com

Kevin Matthews _____

OBJECTIVE   Obtain a position as an advocate in juvenile court

ACCOMPLISHMENTS

- Three years experience leading conflict resolution group for at-risk students
- Recognized as a leader and organizer in high school
- Strong commitment to volunteer work in the community
- Problem-solver, energetic and always willing to learn

EDUCATION

9/98-6/02   High school diploma, Zicon High School, Zicon, CA. GPA – 3.5/4.0

EXPERIENCE

Summers
2001-02   **Camp Counselor,** Wood Acres Residential Camp, Palo Alto, CA

Supervised a group of 14 teenagers for six weeks at a camp for at-risk youth. Responsible for daily camp activities, taught conflict resolution, anger management skills, and focused on self-esteem issues. Awarded Counselor of the Year both summers. Fluent in Spanish.

9/01-6/02   **Office Assistant**, Brock & Smith Law Offices, Zicon, CA

Administrative support for six attorneys in general law practice; worked on implementing new database; answered phones as needed; greeted visitors and made deliveries; scheduled depositions; liaison to the juvenile court system.

9/00-6/01   **Clerk,** Shop & Save, Zicon, CA

Assisted cashier and customers with groceries, responsible for closing store at night, worked overtime every weekend. Part-time.

ADDITIONAL INFORMATION

- Captain, Zicon High School Varsity Soccer Team
- Phone Crisis Counselor, Teen Help-Line, 1999-2000
- Volunteer for team-building athletic events such as rope course and rock climbing.

Here is an example of a resume for a person with no formal work experience:

Nikki Longet

33 La Selva Drive
Brooklyn, N.Y. 07039
(510) 765-0987
kiki@zol.com

Objective: Window designer for retail store

Highlights of Qualifications

- Creative stylist with cutting edge designs
- Self-starter with flexible work style
- Enthusiastic, energetic, and dependable
- Awarded state recognition for set design in high school

Experience

- President of high school drama club, 2000-02
- Lead set-designer, 1999-02
- Costume designer for 8 plays
- Designed bridesmaid dresses for Manhattan dressmaker, 1999-00
- Created Halloween window display for New Wave Beauty Supply, 2001

Volunteer Experience

Summer 2002   **Art Aide**   Camp Mikawaka, Catskills, NY

Assisted art teacher with all projects, including ceramics, painting, arts and crafts for 600 resident campers. Directed innovative art project that involved papier-mache of a small car. Recognition and local news coverage on project.

Education

Graduated June 2002, Brooklyn High School, Brooklyn, NY. GPA: 3.5/4.0, Senior Art Award

Additional Information

Speak fluent Spanish and French
Expert seamstress and quilt designer

Here's an example of a resume for a college graduate:

Brad Gee

2525 Beach Street, Gainesville, FL, (786) 345-9868, BGEE@zol.com

---

OBJECTIVE: To obtain a position as a marketing assistant at American Airlines

EDUCATION:
8/98-6/02   **University of Florida**, Gainesville, FL
                   BS degree in Business Administration
                   Course work included economics, statistics, business management, organizational behavior, and psychology. GPA – 3.6/4.0

EXPERIENCE:
8/01-6/02   **Resident Advisor,** International House, Gainsville, FL
                   Worked as a floor advisor in a 430-freshman student dormitory. Directly responsible for 80 students. Planned floor social activities with the students. Responsible for guiding residents to be responsible young adults. Resolved conflicts and assisted in crisis management. Organized week-long dorm festival; booked musical groups and food vendors; designed posters and marketing plan. Raised $5,000 for resident-life programs.

5/01-8/01   **Salesman**, The Golf Market, Miami, FL

                   Assisted customers with the purchase of golf clubs and golf accessories. Miami Salesman of the Month, July 2001.

5/00-8/00   **Entrepreneur,** Web Page Design, Miami, FL

                   Offered in-home, Web page design to local community and businesses; expanded to set-up service and software instruction. Doubled revenues in two months and sold business before returning to college.

ADDITIONAL INFORMATION:
                   – Speak fluent Spanish and Mandarin
                   – Computer Skills: Excel, PageMaker, PowerPoint
                   – Participant, intramural sports
                   – Enjoy traveling and reading

The Cover Letter

Cover letters provide you with the opportunity to present yourself in a more subjective way to a potential employer. A resume accompanied by a well-written cover letter makes a stronger impact. Cover letters should never be more than one page in length.

Before you write a cover letter:

- ❖ Read the job description carefully and highlight the skills the employer wants.
- ❖ Make a list of the skills in the job description.
- ❖ Make a list of your skills. Match your skills to the ones in the job description.
- ❖ Write an accomplishment statement for each of your skills that match the skills in the job description.
- ❖ Relate your accomplishment statements to the skills the employer is looking for.

For example:

The job requires you to provide customer service to a diverse population.

- ❖ **Your accomplishment statement:** *Communicated with 10 student groups in the county to provide information and peer counseling to non-English speaking students.*

- ❖ **Relate your accomplishment statement to the skill the employer is looking for:** *My experience working with a diverse population involved coordinating student volunteers from all ethnicities to counsel non-English speaking students. I was personally responsible for training 10 peer counselors in conflict resolution and stress management.*

Cover letter format:

Here is an outline to help you write your cover letter:

Personal Information and Salutation:

Date, Name of Interviewer, Title, Address:

Dear Mr./Ms._____, (It is much more effective if you are able to address your letter to the interviewer. If you were not given the person's name, call the human resources department and ask for it.)

Introduction:

State what position you are applying for. Also let the interviewer know if someone suggested you apply for the position. Let them know why you want the job. (I am applying for this position because...)

Content:

Choose the three most important skills you think they are looking for and write your accomplishment statements for each of these. Remember to relate your accomplishment statements to the skills they want.

Content Closing:

Make three strong subjective statements about yourself. For example: *My goal is to be a continuous learner throughout my career, which will provide me with the flexibility to meet all challenges with understanding and knowledge.*

Closing:

A formal statement of commitment to the company or organization. The best way to reach you to set up an interview, and a thank-you for taking the time to review your resume.

Sincerely,

A successful young adult

Sample Cover Letter:

June 24, 2003

Mrs. Jean Kribbs
Strategic Sports Inc.
2345 Cloverleaf Drive
Chapel Hill, NC 78695

Dear Ms. Kribbs,

In response to your recent ad in the *Wall Street Journal* I am applying for the position of Customer Service Representative in the Team Sports Division. I had the opportunity to speak to Ms. Kathy Fila at a recent gathering and she suggested I send my resume to you. I enjoyed talking with Ms. Fila and she thought that my background was an ideal fit for both the position and Strategic Sports Inc. I have the skills and leadership experience needed for a high-volume customer service department.

As stated on my resume, my involvement in team sports has given me the opportunity to enhance my skills in leadership, problem-solving, and time management. Spending three years as captain of two varsity teams required much more than a leadership role. I was also responsible for the financial aspect of outfitting a team. My job included purchasing the highest quality merchandise at the lowest cost, while taking into consideration the company's customer service track record. It is clear that customer service is an important issue when dealing with large quantities of merchandise with exact specifications.

Because of my leadership experience in sports, I had the opportunity to work part time at Sports Emporium. After the first month of employment my manager promoted me to the customer service desk. An average day consisted of helping over 50 customers and handling complaints ranging from simple returns to complex problems. I was consistently praised for my demeanor and problem-solving skills by management and our customers.

It is my personal motto that there is never a problem that can't be solved. I take pride in being a good listener and problem solver. I am confident that I would be an asset to your company and am very excited about the position. Thank you for your time and I look forward to meeting with you in person. I can be reached at (978) 657-4576.

Sincerely,

Job Hunter

Now let's move to the job interview.

Interviewing: The Two-Minute Presentation

Before your first interview, prepare a two-minute presentation using the categories below. Practice this in front of a mirror or with a friend. It will give you an opportunity to observe your body language and ask for constructive feedback. **Summarize the following:**

Your Education:

Your Experience:

Your Accomplishments:

Your Strengths:

Your two-minute presentation will help you to organize your thoughts and build your confidence before an interview. Studies show that when meeting someone for the first time, judgments are formed within four minutes and these judgments will affect subsequent impressions. Many recruiters have commented on candidates leaving a lasting impression in the first two to three minutes of an interview, so make this time count.

The Successful Interview

To be successful when interviewing for a job:

Be Conscientious – prepare as much as you can before the interview. Gather information about the organization, practice interview questions, and arrive early for your interview.

Be Confident – have a self-assured, positive, and upbeat attitude.

Interviewing can be a stressful process, but the most important things to remember are listed below. If you interview and don't receive an offer, it's disappointing, but you need to learn from the experience and move on to the next opportunity.

 Checklist for Interviewing

Be prepared:

✓ With a calendar or notebook devoted to keeping track of interviews, name, location, and time. Always show up at least 15 minutes early for an interview to take a few deep breaths to de-stress and observe your surroundings.

✓ To dress appropriately for the interview. It is acceptable to ask the person who schedules your interview what the appropriate attire will be for the interview.

✓ To develop rapport as soon as you can with the interviewer.

✓ For an open-ended question at the beginning of the interview such as *"Tell us about yourself"* or *"Tell us about your career path."* You may choose to summarize the past five years or give your two-minute presentation (education, experience, accomplishments, strengths) as part of the answer to this question.

✓ To discuss the type of work you want and how your education, experiences, skills, and special talents relate to the job.

✓ For questions asking for examples of a time you used a particular skill or behavior needed for the job. Be prepared with concrete examples of how you previously used the skills advertised for the job.

✓ To describe the organization and know what they do.

✓ To explain why you want to work for them and what you can contribute.

✓ To sound enthusiastic and confident with a positive attitude.

✓ To be honest (never lie on a resume or in an interview).

✓ For surprise questions. Employers ask these questions to find out how you'll react in a stressful situation. It's all right to calmly say, *"Let me take a minute to think about that."*

✓ To always speak well of past employers. Future employers do not want to hear negative remarks because they will think they're next, if you leave the job.

✓ To talk about your future plans. Although the workplace is rapidly changing, employers want to know how long you plan on staying. It is acceptable to say that you will stay as long as the organization provides you with a challenging environment and opportunities to grow in your career.

✓ To let the employer know how much you want the job.

✓ To ask the interviewer well thought-out questions at the end of the interview.

✓ To thank the interviewer, shaking his/her hand and asking for a business card.

After the Interview

Write a thank-you note that day clarifying or enhancing what you said in the interview. Let the interviewer know how much you want the job.

References

Most job interviewers will request references. Choose your references carefully! The following are guidelines for obtaining written and verbal references:

❖ If you are not sure of what a reference will say about you, it is better to ask for a reference in writing, and decide later if you want to use it. Also, ask yourself if you think your reference will communicate better in writing or on the telephone.

❖ Employers generally ask for two to three references. You will need to choose at least two that know you as a student or employee, and a personal reference that can comment on your character.

❖ Obtain written references from teachers and professors while you're enrolled in school. They will have a more recent memory of you, and this will translate to a stronger and more accurate reference.

❖ It is acceptable to provide an outline. You may ask the person to focus on specific skills for a particular job you are applying for.

❖ If you choose to have an employer contact a reference by phone or e-mail, be sure to inform your reference prior to your interview.

❖ Remember to thank your references whether you are offered the job or not. Your references may be able to provide valuable information by telling you what the employer asked about you. This may help you in future interviews.

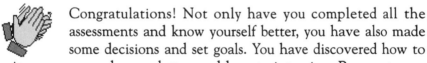 Congratulations! Not only have you completed all the assessments and know yourself better, you have also made some decisions and set goals. You have discovered how to write a resume and cover letter, and how to interview. Be sure to use the next chapter to help you explore some of the careers that interest you. Remember that this book can be used repeatedly as your values, skills, interests, and goals change as you get older. Now that you have good career self-management skills, you are on the road to success!

10

Resources and
the Information Highway

Websites

Websites are constantly changing and what is on the Web today may be gone tomorrow. We have tried to provide a cross-section of resources that you can explore. This list is current as of the publication date.

Exploring Career Assessments

These sites will help you know yourself better. The assessments will give you an in-depth look at your skills, interests, and working styles, and help you explore career options.

www.self-directed-search.com/

> The Self-Directed Search (takes 15 minutes and costs less than $10)

www.myroad.com

> Education and resources (payment is required to use resources)

www.jobhuntersbible.com

> Provided by Richard Bolles, author of *What Color is Your Parachute?*

www.myfuture.com

> Geared towards high school graduates

www.bridges.com

> Education and resources (payment is required to use resources)

www.missouri.edu/~cppcwww/holland.shtml
> Career Interest Game (based on "The Party Exercise" in *What Color is Your Parachute?*)

Exploring Career Resource Information

These sites have general career resources, including how to prepare for the job search, employment opportunities, and resume writing tips.

www.rileyguide.com
> The Riley Guide to career resources

quintcareers.com
> Quintessential Careers (resources)

Exploring Careers and Skills

These sites include jobs and job descriptions, and the skills needed for the job.

www.doleta.gov/programs/onet/
> Department of Labor and Training Administration's *O*NET Online Dictionary of Occupational Titles* identifies over 1,000 job titles and is an updated version of the *Dictionary of Occupational Titles*

www.careerbuilder.com
www.hotjobs.com
www.jobsonline.com
www.sciencecareers.org

Exploring Jobs

If you are looking for a job, these sites list job openings throughout the U.S. and how to apply.

www.aftercollege.com
www.firstjobs.com
www.campuscareercenter.com
www.collegejobs.com
www.jobdirect.com

www.jobtrak.com
www.diversitycareers.com (engineering/information technology)
www.monster.com

Jobs for high school students – part-time and summer jobs:
www.snagajob.com
www.summerjobs.com
www.gsj.Petersons.com

Internships:
www.internshipprograms.com

In addition to the sites above:
Of the Fortune 500 companies, 496 have websites and 462 have jobs posted.

Exploring Market Conditions
These sites list job trends, labor market conditions, and future job outlook.

http://stats.bls.gov/oco/home.htm
   Occupational Outlook Handbook, which provides an overview of labor market conditions
www.wired.com
www.next20years.com

Exploring Wages
These sites list the average wages and benefits for a variety of careers.

www.salary.com
   U.S. Department of Labor, Bureau of Labor Statistics
http://stats.bls.gov
   Includes labor statistics and wage information

Other Resources

One-Stop Career Bookstore, Impact Publications, Manassas Park, VA: www.impactpublications.com. Online bookstore contains down-loadable catalogs and hundreds of career resources (books, videos, software) relevant to young people.

100 Best Careers for the 21st Century (2d Edition), Shelly Field, ARCO, Lawrenceville, NJ, 2000

101 Careers – A Guide to the Fastest Growing Opportunities, Michael Harkavy, John Wiley & Sons, NY, 1999

Cool Careers for Dummies (2nd Edition), Marty Nemko and Paul and Sarah Edwards, John Wiley & Sons, NY, 2001

Cover Letters for Dummies, Joyce Lain Kennedy, John Wiley & Sons, NY, 2000

The Everything Hot Career Book, Ronald Reis, Adams Media Corporation, Avon, MA, 2001

The Job Hunting Guide: Transitioning From College to Career, Ron and Caryl Krannich, Impact Publications, Manassas Park, VA, 2003

Occupational Outlook Handbook, Dictionary of Occupational Titles (DOT) and *Holland Occupational Codes* can all be found in your public library, on the Internet, or at bookstores.

Sweaty Palms: The Neglected Art of Being Interviewed (Revised Ed.), Anthony Medley, Ten Speed Press, Berkeley, CA, 1992

What Color is Your Parachute?, Richard Bolles, Ten Speed Press, Berkeley, CA, 2002

Your First Resume, Ron Fry, Career Press, NJ, 2001

Appendix

Skill Building Cards

Cut on the dotted lines.

PERSUADE ☎	**SELL** ☎	**PROMOTE** 🖌
Convince others to change an attitude or take an action	Convince to make a purchase	Use creativity to persuade through involvement
WRITE ☎	**EDIT** ☎	**PUBLIC** ☎ **SPEAKING**
Demonstrate skill in use of language, grammar, and punctuation	Revise and improve written and verbal material	Enjoy speaking in front of small and large groups
COORDINATE 📁	**PRIORITIZE** 📁	**ORGANIZE** 📁
Arrange sequence and logistics of activities	Set task on urgency and importance	Pull things together in an orderly way
EXPLAIN ☎	**TRAIN** ☎	**SCHEDULE** 📁
Communicate a message or idea in a clear manner	Teach or explain specialized information to others by demonstration	To plan ahead; organize events

PROBLEM SOLVE	ANALYZE	EVALUATE
Find solutions; results oriented	Examine in detail	Assess needs of situation/risks
NEGOTIATE ☎	LISTEN ☎	MEDIATE ☎
Bring about an agreement	Focus carefully on verbal and nonverbal communication	Resolve or settle differences between people
CONSTRUCT	MONITOR 🗁	COUNSEL ☎
Build/operate; physical work	Oversee and regulate flow of work	Facilitate awareness of issues and provide guidance
DEVELOP IDEAS	INVENT	DESIGN
Process information, looking at all possibilities	To produce or create from imagination	Form a plan and carry it out

CONCEPTUALIZE	CHALLENGE LIMITS	CREATE
Form new or creative ideas or theories	Go beyond what is asked or expected	Provide artistic expression
INITIATIVE	**IMPLEMENT**	**CALCULATE**
Take action without direction	Take necessary steps towards goal	Pay attention to detail; work with numbers
MOTIVATE	**DECISION MAKING**	**INTUITION**
Organize people; inspire and stimulate to take action	Choose the best option from alternatives	Rely on insight beyond the senses; gut feeling
INVESTIGATE	**FOLLOW THROUGH**	**TEAM BUILD**
Seek out and study information	Ensure completion	Motivate and manage a group

LEAD	EXPEDITE	SYNTHESIZE
Manage people; manage projects	Speed up results	Integrate ideas and information to solve problems
Make Your Own Card	Make Your Own Card	Make Your Own Card
Make Your Own Card	Make Your Own Card	Make Your Own Card

My Career Road Map

Life Goals:

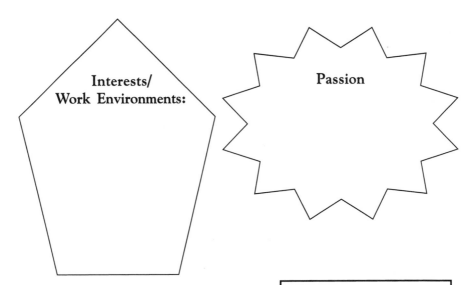

Interests/
Work Environments:

Passion

Motivation:

Four Top Values:

1.

2.

3.

4.

My Career Road Map

Top Five Skills:

1.

2.

3.

4.

5.

Two Strongest Skills Categories:

1.

2.

Top Three Career Choices:

1.

2.

3.

Working Style(s):

Short-Term Goals:

Long-Term Goals:

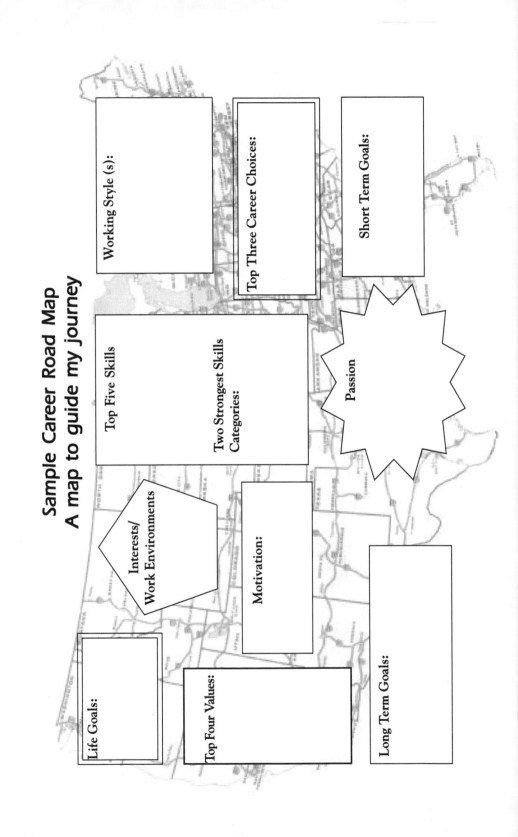

Sample Career Road Map
A map to guide my journey

Working Style (s):

Top Three Career Choices:

Short Term Goals:

Top Five Skills

Two Strongest Skills Categories:

Passion

Interests/
Work Environments

Motivation:

Life Goals:

Top Four Values:

Long Term Goals:

About the Authors

Susan Maltz

Susan has over 20 years experience in education and business as a teacher, writer, career counselor and training specialist. Having a master's degree in Counseling, with a specialization in Career/College Counseling, she has extensive training interpreting the Strong Interest Inventory, Myers Briggs Type Indicator, Career Architect, Skill Scan, and many other assessments. She has developed and led career workshops for organizations in the San Francisco Bay Area for the past 10 years.

Presently Susan is a career management consultant. Previously she was a career counselor in the Career Development Center and Training & Organizational Development at Stanford University.

A Fork in the Road, written with co-author Barbara Grahn, is a result of the numerous inquiries received from high school and college counselors. She hopes the book will help young people pursue their career passions.

Barbara Grahn

Barbara has 13 years experience as a training, organizational development and communication specialist at Stanford University, where her work included writing and designing curricula to help staff develop their careers, writing Web-based training, and designing comprehensive training programs. She also spent over a decade as a program director, teacher, and writer. One of her online courses, "How to Recruit Applicants," won a Cinema in Industry International (CINDY) award in 2001.

Barbara has a master's degree in Public Administration, B.A. in Human Resources Management, and extensive training in art and design. She is also certified to administer various career assessments such as the Career Architect and the Myers Briggs Type Indicator. Her varied careers ranging from a ski instructor, graphic designer to occupational therapist are examples of how young people can mesh their skills and abilities to create jobs that they love.

Currently she is a human resources consultant and artist with a passion for travel. She is working on her second book, an anthology of her adventures in Europe.

Career Resources

Them following Career Resources are available directly from Impact Publications. Full descriptions of each title as well as nine downloadable catalogs, videos, and software can be found on our website: www.impactpublications.com. Complete the following form or list the titles, include shipping (see formula at the end), enclose payment, and send your order to:

IMPACT PUBLICATIONS
9104 Manassas Drive, Suite N
Manassas Park, VA 20111-5211 USA
1-800-361-1055 (orders only)
Tel. 703-361-7300 or Fax 703-335-9486
Email address: info@impactpublications.com
Quick & easy online ordering: www.impactpublications.com

Orders from individuals must be prepaid by check, money order, or major credit card. We accept telephone, fax, and email orders.

Qty.	TITLES	Price	TOTAL
	Featured Title		
_____	A Fork in the Road	$14.95	_____
	College-to-Career Resources		
_____	200 Best Jobs for College Graduates	16.95	_____
_____	America's Top Jobs for College Graduates	15.95	_____
_____	Best Resumes for College Students and New Grads	12.95	_____
_____	College Majors Handbook	24.95	_____
_____	Great Careers in Two Years	19.95	_____
_____	The Job Hunting Guide	14.95	_____
_____	Quick Guide to College Majors and Careers	16.95	_____

Testing and Assessment

_____ Career Tests	12.95	_____
_____ Discover the Best Jobs for You	15.95	_____
_____ Discover What You're Best At	14.00	_____
_____ Do What You Are	18.95	_____
_____ What Type Am I?	14.95	_____

Inspiration and Empowerment

_____ Life Strategies	13.95	_____
_____ Maximum Success	24.95	_____
_____ Seven Habits of Highly Effective People	14.00	_____
_____ Who Moved My Cheese?	19.95	_____

Career Exploration and Job Strategies

_____ 50 Cutting Edge Jobs	15.95	_____
_____ 95 Mistakes Job Seekers Make	13.95	_____
_____ 100 Great Jobs and How to Get Them	17.95	_____
_____ Best Jobs for the 21st Century	19.95	_____
_____ Best Keywords for Resumes, Cover Letters, Interviews	17.95	_____
_____ Change Your Job, Change Your Life (8th Edition)	17.95	_____
_____ Internships	26.95	_____
_____ No One Will Hire Me!	13.95	_____
_____ Occupational Outlook Handbook	16.95	_____
_____ What Color Is Your Parachute?	17.95	_____

Internet Job Search

_____ America's Top Internet Job Sites	19.95	_____
_____ CareerXroads (annual)	26.95	_____
_____ e-Resumes	11.95	_____
_____ Haldane's Best Employment Websites for Professionals	15.95	_____

Resumes and Letters

_____ 201 Dynamite Job Search Letters	19.95	_____
_____ Cover Letters for Dummies	16.99	_____
_____ Haldane's Best Cover Letters for Professionals	15.95	_____
_____ Haldane's Best Resumes for Professionals	15.95	_____
_____ High Impact Resumes and Letters (8th Edition)	19.95	_____
_____ Resumes for Dummies	16.99	_____
_____ The Savvy Resume Writer	12.95	_____

Networking

_____ A Foot in the Door	14.95	_____
_____ How to Work a Room	14.00	_____
_____ Masters of Networking	16.95	_____
_____ The Savvy Networker	13.95	_____

Dress, Image, and Etiquette

_____ Dressing Smart for Men	14.95	_____
_____ Dressing Smart for Women	14.95	_____

Interviews and Salary Negotiations

_____ 101 Dynamite Questions to Ask At Your Job Interview	13.95	_____
_____ Dynamite Salary Negotiations	15.95	_____
_____ Haldane's Best Answers to Tough Interview Questions	15.95	_____
_____ Haldane's Best Salary Tips for Professionals	15.95	_____
_____ Interview for Success (8th Edition)	15.95	_____
_____ Job Interviews for Dummies	16.99	_____
_____ Nail the Job Interview!	13.95	_____
_____ The Savvy Interviewer	10.95	_____

SUBTOTAL	_____
Virginia residents add 4½% sales tax	_____
POSTAGE/HANDLING ($5 for first product and 8% of SUBTOTAL)	_____
8% of SUBTOTAL	$5.00
TOTAL ENCLOSED	_____

SHIP TO:

NAME _____

ADDRESS _____

_____

_____

PAYMENT METHOD:

❑ I enclose check/money order for $ _____ made payable to
IMPACT PUBLICATIONS.

❑ Please charge $ _____ to my credit card:

❑ Visa   ❑ MasterCard   ❑ American Express   ❑ Discover

Card # _____ Expiration date: ___/___

Signature _____

Keep in Touch . . .
On the Web!

www.impactpublications.com
www.winningthejob.com
www.veteransworld.com
www.contentforcareers.com
www.ishoparoundtheworld.com
www.contentfortravel.com